Prophet Muhammad

Peace Be Upon Him

A Summarized Story of God's Last & Final Prophet from Birth to Death

The Sincere Seeker

Introduction to God Sending Messengers and Prophets to Us & Why We Should Study About Prophet Muhammad Peace Be Upon Him

How would one know their role and life purpose unless one receives clear and practical instructions of what God wants and expects of him or her? Here comes the need for Prophethood. Thus, God has sent thousands of Messengers and Prophets to mankind to convey His Message and communicate to us. Every nation on Earth received a Prophet. They all preached the same general Message that there is only one deity worthy of worship. He is the One and Only God, without a partner, son, daughter, or equal. God sent Messengers and Prophets to guide humanity from worshipping created beings and to worship their Creator, the Creator of all things. The Prophets came to teach their people about who their Creator is, how to build a relationship with Him, and how to love Him. The Prophets taught their people that life is only a test, where the successful will enter Paradise eternally, and the unsuccessful will enter the ultimate punishment in the afterlife.

Out of the Infinite Mercy and Love of God, God continued to send Messengers with Books from God to guide humanity-- starting with Prophet Adam, including Noah, Abraham, Ishmael, Jacob, Moses, Prophet Jesus, and Prophet Muhammad, peace be upon them all. Many of the Prophets are found in Jewish and Christian traditions. All the previous Messengers and Books other than the Holy Quran and Prophet Muhammad were sent down only to a specific group of people and were only meant to be followed for a particular period. For example, Prophet Jesus, peace be upon him, was one of God's mightiest Messengers, who was sent down with the same general Message of all the previous Prophets but was only sent to the Children of Israel—the nation that lived before us, as their final Prophet because they were disobeying the commandments of God and veering away from the laws sent down by the previous Messenger, Moses, peace be upon him.

Whenever God would send Messengers with Revelation, after they passed, people would distort and change the Revelations of God. What was pure Revelation from God-- would be polluted with myths, words of men, superstitions, irrational philosophical ideologies, and idol worship. The religion of God was lost in a plethora of religions. Such as how Prophet Jesus, peace be upon him, was sent to reform the previous Message sent before him by the previous Messenger, Moses, peace be upon him. Prophet Muhammad came to reform Prophet Jesus' Message since it was distorted by his followers and did not survive in its original form.

When humanity was in the depth of the dark ages, God the Almighty sent his last and final Messenger to mankind, Prophet Muhamad, peace be upon him, and his final Revelation, the Holy Quran, to redeem humanity. The Holy Quran and the final Messenger, peace be upon him, affirmed everything that was revealed to all the previous Messengers in the past. Unlike the past Messengers and Books, Prophet Muhammad, peace be upon him, was sent to all of humanity, and there will be no Messenger or Prophet after him, nor will there be a Book after the Holy Quran, as both are meant to be followed by all people, not just a particular group of people, nor are they meant for a particular timeframe; both are meant to be followed by everyone until the end of time.

Prophet Muhammad—A summarized story of God's Last and Final Prophet aims to introduce Prophet Muhammad, peace be upon him, derived from early Islamic Sources, helping you better understand who Prophet Muhammad, peace be upon him was and to instill a love for him. Studying the story and life of Prophet Muhammad, peace be upon him, is the best way to develop that love for our Prophet. Studying the life of Prophet Muhammad, peace be upon him, is an obligation given to us by our Creator and helps us better understand God's final Book, the Holy Quran, and its context. We study the life of our final Prophet to derive lessons and morals from his life that would help us better live our lives. God sent him as the perfect role model for us, who taught and demonstrated morality and the highest form of character one could have. We learn about him, so we can follow and emulate him to better ourselves and get closer to God.

In fairness to God, His religion, and yourself, your opinion of Islam, the Holy Quran, and Prophet Muhammad, peace be upon him, should be formed only after a careful study of Islamic sources—the Holy Quran and Hadith—the sayings of Prophet Muhammad, peace be upon him, and not from the media or third-party sources that are non-Muslim in origin.

The Land of Makkah Filled with Idols and Idol Worship

Prophet Muhammad, peace be upon him, was born in Mecca in the year of the Elephant. Mecca is the home of the Kaaba, the first house of worship built on Earth by Prophet Abraham and his son Ismael, peace be upon them. As they were both building the Kaaba, Prophet Abraham, peace be upon him, made a prayer to God that He sends a Prophet in his son Ismael's progeny, who will recite to them God Signs (Verses) and teach them the Book and Wisdom and purify them. This prayer was fulfilled when God sent Prophet Muhammad, peace be upon him, as his last and final Messenger, who was from the progeny of his son Ismael, peace be upon him.

Before Prophet Muhammad became a prophet, many people of Mecca worshipped idols and believed that idols had the power to intercede for them. It was a time full of ignorance, foolishness, and misguidance. At the time, Arabia was a backward nation that did not have infrastructure, monuments, a big civilization, nor a unified government or law and order. They also did not have written literature, and many did not know how to read and write. They had turned the Kaaba, which was dedicated and built for the service of the One True God, Allah, the Glorious, into a place of worship of idols.

Angel Gabriel Splits Open Prophet Muhammad's Chest & Washes His Heart

Sadly, Prophet Muhammad's father died before Prophet Muhammad was born, and he was raised by his mother. At the time, it was a custom for Arabs living in towns to send their young boys to the desert to live with a wet nurse and a Bedouin tribe for a few years, so they could grow stronger and healthier in the harsh climate, learn the ways of the desert, learn from their manners, and it represented a return to their roots. No one originally wanted to take Prophet Muhammad, peace be upon him, as a child to suckle because he was an orphan, and they wouldn't have gotten much money from him. Then Prophet Muhammad's mother, Aminah, eventually sent her child to live with a poor lady named Halima and her husband to spend a couple of years or so in the desert. As soon as they brought on Prophet Muhammad, peace be upon him, as a child, they began to see miracles around them. Their old goat that stopped producing a while back started to produce milk again, and their camel, which was weak and slow, gained strength and speed.

While prophet Muhammad, peace be upon him, was out playing with his foster brothers, Angel Gabriel came down in a human form. The other kids saw him and ran screaming in terror to Halima and her husband, thinking Prophet Muhammad was being abducted. Prophet Muhammad was four years old or so at the time and was fearful but did not scream. Angel Gabriel forced him to the ground as Prophet Muhammad struggled to get lose, but Angel Gabriel overpowered him. Angel Gabriel pulled out a golden utensil with a golden tray filled with Zam-Zam Water and began to split open his chest and take out his heart to wash it. Angel Gabriel took out a black blood clot and threw it away, saying, *'this is Shaytan's (Devil) portion.*' He took out the root of all sins, freeing Prophet Muhammad from evil influences, as Allah, the Glorious, wanted to protect Prophet Muhammad from Shaytan (Devil) and sins. He then stitched him back up.

Halima and her husband rushed over to Prophet Muhammad, whose face was pale from fear. Halimah's husband comforted him with a hug and took him in to rest. They realized that there was something special with this boy and decided it was best to return him to his mother, Aminah in Mecca. He lived with her for a short period, and then sadly, she passed away from illness on her way back from the city of Yathrib, later to be called Medina.

His loving grandfather Abdul Muttalib ended up raising him for 2 years. He loved Prophet Muhammad more than he loved his own children. Prophet Muhammad, peace be upon him, would watch and learn from his grandfather what it would be like to be the leader of the Arabs as his grandfather was the most prestigious and senior statemen of Quraish, the ruling tribe and custodians of Mecca.

At the age of 8, Prophet Muhammad's grandfather passes away, and the charge of Prophet Muhammad was passed down to his uncle Abu Talib, who was the brother of Prophet Muhammad's father. His uncle also loved and preferred him over his children. Being an orphan taught Prophet Muhammad wisdom and helped mature him quickly, and he learned to be independent. He experienced and learned from his early hardships, and it helped prepare him to bear the tough life and battles he would later go through.

Prophet Muhammad's Marriage to His Wife, Khadijah, Peace be Upon Her

As a young man, Prophet Muhammad worked as a shepherd for the people of Mecca, bringing him a small wage just like past Prophets who were shepherds in their time. Working as a shepherd taught Prophet Muhmmad the art of patience and how to deal with and manage sheep with different personalities, which would help a future leader deal with people with different personalities. Prophet Muhammad, peace be upon him, did not grow up as many others did consuming alcohol and other harmful things for the soul or body, nor did he ever worship idols. He grew up establishing a reputation for himself as an honest and trustworthy person. In his early twenties, due to his maturity and character, he was invited to participate in the tribe's legislative body with the leaders of the tribe. He continued to work as a shepherd for more people.

Khadijah, peace be upon her, was the wealthiest businesswoman in Makkah, who inherited a lot of money from her husband, who passed away. She was known for her pureness, nobility, wisdom, and fortune. Her sister had a herd of camels and hired Prophet Muhmmad, along with another person. When the job was complete, the other person who was hired with Prophet Muhmmad told Prophet Muhammad that they should go pick up their wages for the job. Prophet Muhammad asked him if he could go alone because he was too shy. Khadijah heard her sister praise Prophet Muhammad for his nobility, integrity, kindness, good manners, shyness, and other good qualities.

Since Khadijah, peace be upon her, was a lady, she was not able to participate in transactions and trades in person and, instead, invested in business partnerships that would go to Syria and Yemen by sending men to go on her behalf and pay them a fraction of the profits. However, she would often find herself receiving fewer profits than she should have because the men that she hired would pocket some of the profits. She decided to employ Prophet Muhammad to take her merchandise to Syria, even though he was inexperienced. Before he accepted the job, he asked his uncle for permission, who said yes. When Prophet Muhammad returned to Makkah, she noticed triple the profits and blessings than she used to get. She was very impressed with his character and dealings.

Prophet Muhammad, peace be upon him, made a reputation for being honest, reliable, modest, and good character, even though this was rare to find in Makkah at the time. He was known to his community as *'the truthful, the trustworthy'* and was trusted by everyone in his community, even by those who did not like him.

Khadijah, peace be upon her, was twice widowed, and many men from her tribe had proposed marriage to her, yet she did not accept any proposals, nor was she thinking about getting remarried. Khadijah's older friend approached Prophet Muhammad and hinted that Khadijah was interested in marrying him. Khadijah was older than Prophet Muhammad, and Prophet Muhammad was around 25 years old. Prophet Muhammad was interested in marrying Khadijah, so he asked permission from his uncle, who thought it was a good idea because of the type of person Khadijah was. They had a beautiful marriage full of love and understanding. Khadijah supported Prophet Muhammad through his tough years. They had six children together; three sons and three daughters. All the males died in childhood.

His wife Khadijah, peace be upon her, gifted Prophet Muhammad a young servant named Zaid who had been brought as a captive to Mecca and sold to Khadijah, peace be upon her.

When Zaid's father heard that his son Zaid was in possession of Prophet Muhammad, he traveled to Mecca to offer Prophet Muhmmad a large amount for his son. Prophet Muhammad, peace be upon him, told Zaid's father that if Zaid agrees to go back with him, he can take him for no charge. Zaid chose to stay with Prophet Muhmmad because they loved each other so much, and he treated him like his own son. As soon as Prophet Muhammad, peace be upon him, heard that Zaid chose to stay, he grabbed Zaid by his hand and walked over to the black stone of the Kaaba and publicly announced that he had adopted Zaid. Zaid's father traveled back home, content that his son was in good hands and happy.

Rebuilding of the Kaaba After the Flood

At the age of 35, a flood destroyed the Kaaba, and it needed to be rebuilt. Each tribe in Mecca was responsible for rebuilding a part of the Kaaba. The Black Stone, a holy, sacred object that was sent down from Paradise within the Kaaba was removed for the renovation and needed to be placed back into the Kaaba. The leaders of Mecca were in disagreement for 5 days, and blood was almost shed, trying to determine which clan would have the honor of placing the Black Stone back in its original place. They concluded that the next man that walked in would choose who would place the Black Stone back to its original place.

That person turned out to be Prophet Muhammad, peace be upon him. Instead of choosing a particular person or clan to place the Black Stone back in its original place, Prophet Muhammad, peace be upon him, asked for a cloth in which he placed the Black Stone in the center and had the leader of each clan hold a corner of the cloth and carry it back to the Kaaba together. Then Prophet Muhammad, peace be upon him, set the Back Stone with his two hands in its original place, and all the clans were satisfied.

This demonstrated and symbolized the future of Prophet Muhammad, peace be upon him, and how he would soon unify the Arab tribes under one banner of Islam, just like he unified them at this moment without any conflict or bloodshed. It also demonstrated and symbolized that Prophet Muhammad, peace be upon him, would be the one to unify the religion of Prophet Abraham, peace be upon him, after it was destroyed.

Angel Gabriel Comes Down to Prophet Muhammad to Reveal the First Verses of the Holy Quran

As Prophet Muhammad, peace be upon him, would walk, he would hear rocks and stones greet him. Prophet Muhammad, peace be upon him, would also see pleasant dreams, which would prove to become true when he awoke. Prophet Muhammad had the habit of secluding himself in a cave called Hira because he felt something was missing in his life, and he didn't know what it was. Even though he had a good wife and children, a good life, and good status in society, he felt something was missing. He knew having these alone does not bring happiness. He would go to Cave Hira to contemplate about life, this Universe, and this world. He would meditate, ponder, reflect deeply, and wonder how to worship Allah.

When Prophet Muhammad, peace be upon him, was 40 years old, during the month of Ramadan, Angel Gabriel startled Prophet Muhammad in the cave and demanded that he reads, even though he did not know how to read or write. Prophet Muhammad, peace be upon him, replied, *'I do not know how to read.'* Then Angel Gabriel squeezed Prophet Muhammad so tight it caused him to lose all his energy. Angel Gabriel repeated the request two more times in which Prophet Muhammad had the same response. Angel Gabriel grasped Prophet Muhammad with overwhelming force, then released him again. Then the first Recitation of the Holy Quran was revealed to Prophet Muhammad via Angel Gabriel; *'Recite in the name of your*

Lord who created -Created man from a clinging substance. Recite, and your Lord is the Most Generous -Who taught by the pen -Taught man that which he knew not' (Quran 96:1-5) It was the beginning of Allah the Glorious first Revelation sent via the Angel Gabriel to humanity meant until the end of times.

Prophet Muhammad hurried home to his supportive wife in fear and asked her to cover him. She quickly covered him with a cloak. When Prophet Muhammad calmed a bit, he told her what had happened and that he was scared. She replied, comforting her husband with the following statement, *'God will never humiliate you, as you are good to your family, you take on other people's burden, and help the needy!'*

Then Khadijah takes Prophet Muhamad to her cousin Waraqah, a Biblical Scholar at the time, and told him what had happened. He then realized that Prophet Muhammad is the awaited Prophet in which the Gospel prophesied and concluded that the one that visited Prophet Muhammad was indeed Angel Gabriel.

Prophet Muhammad continued to receive Revelations for the remainder of his life. These Revelations were memorized and written down by the Prophet's companions and were later compiled to make up the Holy Quran which we have today.

Prophet Muhammad Spreads & Preaches Islam Privately, then Publicly

Prophet Muhammad, peace be upon him, was walking and heard a sound, so he looked up in the Heavens and saw Angel Gabriel sitting on a throne in the Heavens and Earth. Prophet Muhammad was terrified again and hurried home to his wife and asked her to cover him. Then Angel Gabriel revealed the second Revelation of the Holy Quran: *"O, you who covers himself [with a garment], Arise and warn, And your Lord glorify, And your clothing purify, And uncleanliness avoid, And do not confer favor to acquire more, But for your Lord be patient" (Quran 74:1-7)*.

For the first three years, Prophet Muhammad started to spread the Message of Islam privately one-on-one to his close family and friends that he thought would be interested in Islam-- freeing them from the practices of their forefathers and the worship of false gods and did not publicize the Message yet. Prophet Muhammad, peace be upon him, taught and preached that there is Only One True God that deserves to be worshipped and Praised, and all other gods, including idols, are false and are only creations of God, not the actual Creator Himself. He taught them that the one that believes in God and lives a righteous life would live a good life in this world and would be awarded Paradise in the afterlife, in which they would live forever. He also warned those who do not believe in God that they would live a bad life in this world and be punished severely in the next world.

The first person to accept the Message of Islam was his wife Khadija, as well as her cousin Waraqah. The first slave to convert was Zaid, the first child to convert was his cousin Ali bin Abi Talib, and the first free adult to convert was his best friend Abu Bakr As-Siddiq, peace be upon them all.

After three years of secretly struggling to spread Islam to his close companions, Prophet Muhammad converted 30 people. Then God instructed Prophet Muhammad to publicize and spread the Message of Islam to the public and to speak out against idolatry and the worship of false gods to the people of Mecca, then later to spread the Message beyond Mecca. Khadijah, peace be upon her, supported the rise of Islam with her wealth by providing food, water, and medicine for the Muslims.

The Idol-Worshippers of Mecca Persecute and Harass the Believers

Prophet Muhammad and his early followers,' peace be upon them, were being persecuted and harassed by the idol worshippers of their tribe, the Quraishi tribe in Mecca. The idol-worshippers would degrade them, scoff at them, and ridicule them. They would call Prophet Muhmmad a madman, a liar, a sorcerer, a magician, and one that is possessed by a Jinn. They would prevent Prophet Muhammad and the Muslims from praying at Allah's Sacred House, the Kaaba, and they would cover them in dirt and filth when praying.

They couldn't kill Prophet Muhammad personally as he was the grandson of Abdul Muttalib—who was amongst the elites of the tribe of Banu Hashim, and it was a strict custom and a law of theirs to protect noble blood.

Despite all the ridicule, Prophet Muhammad continued to preach and teach the Message of Islam to the Arabs of Mecca in a gentle manner. He warned them that if they continued to worship other gods besides Allah and not follow the path of Allah, they would face a serious punishment like the previous nations did, who also disobeyed Allah and His Messengers.

The idol-worshippers of Mecca told Prophet Muhammad if you are really a Prophet of God, why don't you split the moon in half, proving you are a Prophet? Prophet Muhammad, peace be upon him, responded, if I do this with the will of God, will you then believe I am a Prophet? They answered, yes! Prophet Muhammad then pointed to the moon, and in front of their eyes, the moon split in half. However, Mecca's idol-worshippers arrogantly turned around, saying that he'd blinded them to the truth and had bewitched their eyes.

As the small number of Muslims started to grow in number, the idol worshippers of Quraish became alarmed and worried that their power and prestige were at risk. They were the custodians of the idols in Mecca and would receive money from them, which was also at risk now that Prophet Muhammad and the Muslims were preaching to remove them. The non-believers offered Prophet Muhammad money, honor, and high rank as a leader in an attempt to stop him from spreading Islam, which, of course, he rejected. He was not interested in any of that and only wanted to spread Allah's Message to the people.

The people of Quraish plotted to stop the Muslims from growing by organizing a full-scale opposition campaign. They tortured their family members that accepted Islam as their religion and way of life.

When the persecution by the people of Quraish grew more severe and unbearable, some of the Muslims decided to migrate to Abyssinia (Ethiopia) to seek refuge in the Kingdom of the Christian King of Abyssinia, who was a fair and righteous king that would welcome the Muslims. This was known as the first Hijrah (Migration) of the Muslims. Later, more Muslims who were being harassed would join them.

The Idol-Worshippers of Mecca Prostrate to Allah

In Ramadan, Prophet Muhammad recited Surah An-Najm (The Chapter of the Star) from the Holy Quran to a gathering that included some of the high-ranked idol-worshippers from the tribe of Quraish in Mecca. The awe-inspiring words of Allah impacted the listeners' hearts, and the unbelievers were overwhelmed in emotion and could not help themselves but unconsciously bowed down in prostration. The idol-worshippers that were not present got upset when they heard what happened. The idol-worshippers that prostrated made up lies about what happened to justify why they prostrated.

News of this incident was highly exaggerated and misreported to the Muslims who migrated to Abyssinia, which led them to think that the idol-worshippers of Mecca had accepted Islam, so they made their way back to Mecca. As the Muslims got close to Mecca, they found out that this rumor was not true. When they arrived at Makkah, some of the Muslims traveled back to Abyssinia. It was harder for them to flee back to Abyssinia again now that the idol-worshippers were more aware. This time around, the Muslims that migrated to Abyssinia was four times more than the first migration.

Some of the big names of Makkah accepted Islam, including Umar ibn Al-Khattab and Hamza ibn Abdul-Muttalib, the Prophet's uncle, peace be upon them both. With the Muslims growing and some big names converting to Islam, this scared the idol-worshippers of Makkah. After many attempts to stop Prophet Muhammad and the believers from spreading Islam, and after a few attempts trying to convince the Prophet's uncle Abu Talib, who raised the Prophet and had a high rank in the tribe, to tell his nephew to stop, the non-believers resorted to their old ways of persecuting and torturing the Muslims in a more severe way than they did the first time.

The idol-worshippers of Makkah held a meeting and decided not to involve any of the Muslims in any inter-marriage or have any business dealings with any of them, including Abu Talib, the Prophet's uncle, even though he had not accepted Islam-- just simply because he did not agree to stop Prophet Muhammad, peace be upon him. The Muslims had to flee to an abandoned valley for a couple of years due to the boycott, as the idol-worshippers of Quraish wouldn't sell them food, water, and clothes. When they moved to the abandoned valley, they did not have many resources, which was not easy. Later, they were able to return to Mecca.

The Year of the Sorrow

In the following year, back to back to back calamities hit Prophet Muhammad within two months. Prophet Muhammad's beloved uncle Abu Talib, who had been protecting him against his enemies, felt sick and was reaching his death. When Abu Talib was about to die, Prophet Muhammad entered the room while Abu Jahl was there, the enemy of Islam, along with another. Prophet Muhammad said to his uncle, Abu Talib, *'O My Uncle, say there is no deity worthy of worship except Allah!'* Abu Talib was about to say it, but every time he was about to say it, Abu Jahl would say, *'Are you going to leave the religion of your father?'* Later, Abu Talib sadly passed without converting to Islam.

About forty days after that, the Prophet's wife Khadijah, peace be upon her, who was huge support for him, died as well. It was known as the year of the sorrow, a very tough and sad year for the Prophet, peace be upon him. Prophet Muhammad was not seen smiling for months.

Later, Prophet Muhammad and his adopted son Zaid, traveled to a town called Taif to spread the Message of Islam and to find protection and support from another city-- only to receive disrespect and refusal. They also pelted them with stones, leaving them bloody and then asked them to return to Mecca. It was Prophet Muhammad's most difficult day of his life.

Prophet Muhammad needed to migrate to another city for protection. He was secretly reaching out to different tribes on the outskirts of Mecca to spread the Message of Allah and find a tribe that would welcome him in their land and support him. Prophet Muhammad approached five people from the city of Yathrib (later to be called Medina) and conveyed the Message of God to them. They went back to their city and spread the news among their people that a Prophet had arisen among the Arabs, who was to call them to God and put an end to the worship of their false gods. Later, Prophet Muhammad concluded a marriage contract with Aishah, peace be upon her.

Prophet Muhammad's Night Journey and Ascension

In the twelfth year of Prophet Muhammad's mission, Angel Gabriel descended down to Prophet Muhammad and opened his chest up once again to remove his heart and wash it-- to strengthen him to what he was about to see and experience, known as the Night Journey and Ascension (Isra wal Miraj in Arabic). Prophet Muhammad, peace be upon him, took a night journey from Masjid Al-Haram in Mecca to Masjid Al-Aqsa in Jerusalem, on a speedy beast, which was pure white called Al-Buraq, in the company of the Archangel Gabriel. When they reached their destination, they tied the beast to a ring in the gate of the Mosque. Prophet Muhammad prayed two units of prayer and turned around and found all the Prophets behind him. He led the Prophets in Prayer.

After visiting Masjid Al-Aqsa, they ascended physically to the Heavens. Angel Gabriel set out with Prophet Muhammad on the same horse till they reached the first heaven. When they reached the gate, the Guardian Angel asked, *'who is it?'* Angel Gabriel answered, *'it's Gabriel.'* Then the voice asked, *'Who are you with?'* In which Angel Gabriel responded, *'Muhammad.'* The voice asked, *'Has Muhammad been called for?'* Angel Gabriel responded, *'Yes.'* The voice responded, *'Then he is welcome, what an excellent visit this is!'* Then the gate opened. Prophet Muhammad saw Prophet Adam there in the first Heaven.

Angel Gabriel introduced Prophet Adam to Prophet Muhammad, peace be upon them both. *'This is your father, Adam, send him your greetings,'* said Angel Gabriel to Prophet Muhammad. Prophet Muhammad greeted Prophet Adam. Prophet Adam responded with a greeting and said, *'You are welcomed, O pious son and pious Prophet.'*

Then Angel Gabriel and Prophet Muhammad ascended to the second Heaven, then the third, and then the fourth, fifth, sixth, and seventh Heaven, where they saw and greeted other Prophets of God, including Prophet John (Yahya), and Jesus (Isa), Joseph, Enoch (Idris), and Aaron (Harun), Moses, and Abraham, peace be upon them all.

Then Prophet Muhammad was carried to Sidrat-al-Muntaha, the Remotest Lote-Tree, where its fruits are like jugs, and its leaves are as big as elephant ears. He was also shown Al-Bait-al-Ma'mûr (The Much Frequented House), which is located above the Ka'ba in the Seventh Heaven, which has a group of 70,000 angels circle it, leave, and never to return-- being followed by the next group of 70,000 Angels and will continue like this until the Day of Judgment. Prophet Muhammad, peace be upon him, was then presented to the Divine Presence of Allah, the Glorious, where Allah issued the five daily prayers to us. When Prophet Muhammad, peace be upon him, returned, some of the people believed in his story, as they were well aware of the Power and Ability of God, and some did not believe him and mocked him, including one of the biggest enemies of Islam, Abu Jahl.

The Muslims Migrate to the City of Medina

Later, the people of Yathrib, who spoke to Prophet Muhammad the year prior, had converted to Islam and returned to Prophet Muhammad, promising to support him, and invited him to their city, which Prophet Muhammad agreed to. Prophet Muhammad, peace be upon him, had family in the city of Yathrib and had traveled there with his mother when he was younger right before she passed away. Now that the Muslims had a place to live without persecution, many of the Muslims migrated to Yathrib, which was later named Medina. About one hundred families quietly migrated from Mecca to Medina secretly. Many of the Muslim immigrants that traveled to Abyssinia prior also migrated to Medina. The Prophet, his cousin Ali, and his friend Abu Bakr remained in Mecca for the time being. The Prophet was waiting for instructions from God before migrating.

The idol-worshippers of Mecca feared the growth and power of the Muslims. They saw them as a threat to their religion and began to think of ways to kill Prophet Muhammad, peace be upon him, even though that would go against their laws, as it was unheard of to kill someone of their own blood-- especially in the sacred land from Mecca. Each tribe sent one of their young men to the Prophet's house to kill him. Then Angel Gabriel was sent down to Prophet Muhammad to let him know what the idol-worshippers of Mecca were plotting. Angel Gabriel also informed Prophet Muhammad that he has Allah's permission to leave Makkah. The enemies of the Prophet surrounded his house, but Allah covered their eyes and blinded them, allowing Prophet Muhammad to escape while reciting Verses from Chapter Yaseen from the Holy Quran. Prophet Muhammad and his companion Abu Bakr fled to a cave named Thor, where they spent 3 days.

The idol-worshippers hired someone to trace the footsteps of Prophet Muhammad to figure out where he went. He led them to the cave that they were in. So, the idol-worshippers sent in their troops to the cave, and Abu Jahl was with them. The Prophet's companion, Abu Bakr, whispered to Prophet Muhammad that all they needed to do was look down, and they would see them. Then Prophet Muhammad responded, *'O Abu Bakr, what do you think of two people, Allah is the third of them?'* The idol-worshippers of Mecca failed to find Prophet Muhammad and his companion, so they left and offered anyone that finds Prophet Muhammad and his companion a hundred camels in blood money-- if they bring them dead or alive. But Prophet Muhammad and his companion Abu Bakr fled to Medina.

Upon arrival to Medina, Prophet Muhammad's first task was to build a Mosque called Masjid Quba in the very site where his camel knelt down. It was land owned by two orphans, and Prophet Muhammad purchased the land from them. Prophet Muhammad helped his companions build this Mosque by carrying bricks and stones while reciting Verses of the Holy Quran. With God & the Quran's Guidance, Prophet Muhammad, peace be upon him, taught and preached the Islamic way of life to his companions in Medina. He was their guide, teacher, judge, consoler, arbitrator, adviser, and father-figure to the new community in Medina.

The migration of the Muslims to Medina is known as *'The Hijra'* in Arabic and was later adopted as the start of the

Muslim calendar. Those who emigrated from Mecca to Medina earned the title of *Muhajireen (The Emigrants).* The Muslims that were living in Medina and welcomed and supported the Emigrants adopted the title of *'The Ansar' (The Helpers).* Prophet Muhammad, peace be upon him, made a pact of mutual religious solidarity between both Muslim groups.

Two Arab tribes ruled Medina called *The Aws* and *The Khazraj*-- who were constantly fighting among themselves for many years, and many of their seniors had died-- soon came to peace when Prophet Muhammad entered their city. Prophet Muhammad started to enter into treaties with other tribes living around them. Prophet Muhammad made a pact between all the tribes of Medina, including the Jewish tribes and idol-worshipping tribes living in the area, that they would all support one another in defending the city against an attack. For the first time, the Muslims had their own state.

After about a year and a half after the Muslims migrated to Medina, the Qibla (the direction in which Muslims pray) was changed after Prophet Muhammad, peace be upon him, made a dua (prayer supplication) to Allah, the Glorious, to change the direction from Masjid Al-Aqsa to the Kaaba.

The Battle of Badr | Supported with Angels

Towards the second year of the Muslims migrating to Medina, the idol-worshippers of Mecca began a series of hostile acts against the Muslims living in Medina. They sent men to destroy the Muslim's fruit trees and carry away their flocks. Soon, permission was given by God to Prophet Muhammad and the Muslims to fight back to protect themselves and their families because they had been wronged by the oppressive idol-worshippers, who'd kicked them out of their homes in Mecca and denied them their basic freedoms and rights. Prophet Muhammad and the Muslims prepared their state of military.

A force of about 1,300 men of Mecca's idol-worshippers marched under their leader Abu Jahl, the great enemy of Islam, towards Medina and the Muslims to attack them. Prophet Muhammad, peace be upon him, had sent scouts and learned their enemies were on their way to kill them.

About 313 of the Muslims gathered in the plains of Badr, located near the sea between Mecca and Medina, with only seventy camels and three horses. They had their men ride in turns since they did not have enough camels. This battle is known as the Battle of Badr because it occurred in the Valley of Badr. The two armies met in the month of Ramadan. Prophet Muhammad, peace be upon him, spent the whole night in prayer and supplication to God, the Most-Merciful, that his small Muslim army would not be destroyed. As the two armies met in the Valley of Badr,

Allah, the Glorious, supported the Muslims with 1,000 Angels that came down to fight alongside them. With the help of the Angels that God sent down, the Muslims were able to defeat the idol-worshippers.

The battle ended with the idol-worshippers of Mecca fleeing back to Mecca with a great loss. Several of their chiefs and leaders were killed, including Abu Jahl. Seventy of the idol-worshippers of Mecca were killed while only 15 Muslims died as martyrs. The idol-worshippers also had 70 of their people taken as prisoners of war, who remained in the hands of the Muslims. They were treated with great humanity, as Prophet Muhammad had strict orders to treat the prisoners of war with kindness, even though they tried to kill them. At this time, it was unheard of to treat prisoners of war this way. The Muslims would have the prisoners of war ride their animals while they would walk. The Muslims would also share their food with the prisoners of war, even though they had little of it.

The division of the spoils of war created some disagreement between the Muslims. Prophet Muhammad divided it equally among his people. Later, a Qur'an Revelation came down, ruling on how to divide the spoils of war going forward. Islam gained new converts in Medina and was growing.

After the Battle of Badr, a group of hypocrites emerged. In Mecca, there was no reason for one to become a hypocrite pretending to be Muslim as Islam was in the beginning phase and was weak and oppressed. Only a sincere and genuine person would convert to Islam. But later, when the Muslims migrated to Medina and Islam started to grow in number and power, one that would not declare himself a Muslim, would remain on the fringe of society and become amongst the few. Therefore, a group that still believed in idolatry in their hearts and did not believe or care for the Message of Islam, felt like they had no other option but to pretend they were Muslim, even though in their heart, they were not. Some pretended to become Muslim for political and economic gains. The hypocrites had a hatred for Prophet Muhammad and Islam because they were leaders of the city of Yathrib and had to give up leadership when Prophet Muhammad and Islam emerged in their city.

The Battle Uhud | Muslims Archers Leave their Post

The Battle of Badr left Mecca's idol-worshippers grieving from their loss, and they wanted to seek revenge against the Muslims. Later, another battle occurred between the idol-worshippers of Mecca and the Muslims, called the Battle of Uhud, a hill about 4-miles to the north of the city of Medina. The idol-worshippers made better preparations this time to attack and beat the Muslims. The idol-worshippers gathered an army of 3,000 men, 200 horses, and even two dozen of their women under their current leader, Abu Sufyan. The Muslims were less in number at around 1,000 men and only 1 horse. Later, the Muslims were abandoned by 300 of the hypocrites of the Muslims, so the number of Muslims went down to 700 men instead of 1,000.

Prophet Muhammad suggested that the Muslims stay within the town to receive the idol-worshippers from there since they were outnumbered, but some of his companions advised they march out against the idol-worshippers.

Prophet Muhammad and the Muslims offered their prayers in the morning, then advanced to the plains to prepare for battle. When they reached the place of battle, Prophet Muhammad positioned some of his men to have their backs toward the hill. Prophet Muhammad then placed fifty Muslim archers on top of the hill behind the Muslim troops to prevent the idol-worshippers from surrounding the Muslims, and so they could have a good view from afar. Prophet Muhammad, peace be upon him, commanded the

Muslim archers on top of the hill not to leave their post no matter what happens, even if they see the idol-worshipers fleeing, and he was very strict and clear about that.

Later, the Muslims were winning the battle, and it appeared the Muslims had defeated the idol-worshippers. The Muslims archers on top of the hill saw that the idol-worshippers fleeing the battlefield and had left some of their stuff behind. The Muslim archers on top of the hill began to dispute among themselves if they should go down and grab what the idol-worshippers had left behind. The leader of the Muslim archers that Prophet Muhammad appointed asked them, *'Have you forgotten what Prophet Muhammad told us?'*

Fifty Muslim archers that were instructed not to leave their post left their position, except for ten of them. This allowed the idol-worshippers of Mecca to come back around, climb the hill, attack the Muslims, surround and surprise them from the back, and create complete disorder which resulted in the Muslims losing.

Prophet Muhammad, peace be upon him, called his companions back, but only twelve men remained with the Prophet. Prophet Muhamad was struck down by stones, wounded in the face by two arrows, and fell unconscious. About seventy or seventy-five of the Muslims were killed in this battle, and among them was the Prophet's uncle Hamza, peace be upon them all. Of the idol worshippers, twenty-two men died.

The Betrayal of the Jewish Tribes of Medina

After the Muslims lost the Battle of Uhud, the Muslims were treated differently by the Jewish and Arab tribes in Medina. The Jewish tribe of Banu Qaynuqa increased their hostility against the Muslims. They told Prophet Muhammad, peace be upon him when he came to remind them of their treaty not to be deceived over their victory in the Battle of Badr against the idol-worshippers of Quraish since they had little understanding of the art of war. They also added if the Muslims had fought them, they would see how war really was and how fierce of an enemy they were. They also broke the treaty with the Muslims by killing a Muslim in the marketplace. So, Prophet Muhammad, peace be upon him, ended the treaty with them and expelled them from the city by giving them three days to pack their stuff and leave.

Another Jewish tribe in Medina called Bani Nadhir also broke their treaty with the Muslims by attempting to kill Prophet Muhammad, peace be upon him, by asking him to sit in a particular place where they tried to drop a big piece of a wall of a fortress. But Angel Gabriel told Prophet Muhammad what they were plotting, and he got up. Prophet Muhammad had no other choice but to expel this Jewish Tribe from Medina as well for their evil actions and betrayal. Prophet Muhammad asked them to grab all their belongings and leave the city, which they did and moved to a neighboring city named Khaybar.

The Battle of the Trench

Soon, the Jewish tribe of Bani Nadhir that were expelled from their homes because of what they had done to the Muslims wanted to get the land back they'd lost and wanted to wipe out the Muslims. They started to recruit and negotiate alliances with other tribes, including the idol-worshippers of Mecca. They also negotiated with the hypocrites of the Muslims to help them attack the Muslims. The enemies of Islam also went to the biggest Bedouin tribe in the area and bribed them with half of their produce in Khaybar for 1-year as payment if they would join them in battle, which they accepted.

In the fifth year of the Muslims migrating to Medina, Abu Sufyan, the leader of the non-believers, set out with 10,000 men from different tribes. This was the greatest army ever seen in the Arabian Peninsula at the time. The Muslims only had about 2,500-3,000 men, so they were greatly outnumbered once again.

This battle was called the *Battle of Al-Ahzab,* which translates to *The Battle of the Confederates or Groups* because different groups of enemies of Islam got together to attack the Muslims. This battle is also known as the Battle of the Trench.

The Muslims needed a plan to defend themselves against the enemies of Islam. One of the companions, Salman the Persian, peace be upon him, suggested digging a deep ditch around the city, making it difficult for the enemies to cross over quickly. They did not need to dig through the entire city since part of the city of Medina was covered with volcanic rock formations, mountains, houses tightly congested together, and large plantations of date trees, making it impossible for large armies to get through. Digging a trench was a technique used by the Persians, and it was unheard of to the Arabs.

All the Muslims, including Prophet Muhammad and children, worked together to dig the trenches using only a shovel each. The trench was about thirteen feet wide and two kilometers long and took somewhere around 1-2 weeks to dig. Once the trench had been dug, they waited for the enemies to come. When they arrived, the enemies of Islam saw the ditch and were surprised. The enemies of Islam realized they would not be able to jump past the ditch with their animals because of its width, and they would not be able to climb down the ditch with their animals either. They would have to go down the ditch individually, putting themselves at risk of easily getting hit by the Muslims as they climbed down.

The enemies of Islam camped outside the trenches in their tents to discuss their next move. Then the enemies decided to send someone to the Jewish Tribe living inside Medina and ask them to join and help them attack the Muslims from inside. The Jewish tribe living inside initially refused at first because of their treaty with the Muslims. But after being tempted, they agreed to join the enemies and attack the Muslims from inside while the others attacked the Muslims from the outside.

Once the Muslims heard the Jewish tribe from inside had betrayed the Muslims, the Muslims panicked and got terrified as they were about to be attacked from both the inside and outside of the city. Prophet Muhammad, peace be upon him, sent all the women and kids to the house of one of the companions who was blind.

Then God the Almighty, sent down strong winds, a sandstorm, which has never hit the city of Medina like this before. The enemy's pots of food were blown and spilled all over, and it became very difficult to see anything. The enemies had no other choice but to flee, which they did, and they were defeated without a war. The Muslims then eliminated the Jewish tribe of Banu Qurayza that betrayed the Muslims, living inside the city of Medina.

The Treaty of Hudaybiyyah

Prophet Muhammad had a dream in which he saw himself entering Makkah unopposed, doing tawaf (circling the Kaaba) in ihram, and shaving his hair. He interpreted this dream to mean he would be performing Umrah (lesser pilgrimage). So, Prophet Muhammad and 1,400 of his companions went forth to perform Umrah in Mecca.

As Prophet Muhammad and his companions were traveling to perform Umrah, as they drew near, they were warned that the idol-worshippers of Quraish had sworn to prevent Prophet Muhammad and the Muslims from entering Makkah. Prophet Muhammad decided to take a detour, taking another route to bypass the troops of Khalid bin Waleed. Then God the Almighty caused the Prophet's camel to camp at a plain called Hudaybiyyah.

Prophet Muhammad sent an emissary to the idol-worshippers of Mecca to let them know that they were here peacefully on a mission for Umrah. The idol-worshippers of Mecca also sent emissaries to the Muslims. Then Prophet Muhammad sent Uthman Bin Affan because of his kinship with the leaders of Quraish in Mecca. Uthman Bin Affan negotiated with Abu Sufiyan and other leaders of the idol-worshippers of Mecca. The meeting took longer than expected. Then rumors started to spread that Uthman Bin Affan had been killed. Prophet Muhammad, who was sitting under a tree, and the Muslims made an oath that they would go to Mecca to seek revenge, and no matter what happens, they would not flee. A little while later, they found out that Uthman Bin Affan had not been killed.

Soon, Prophet Muhammad explained to the idol-worshippers of Quraish that they had only come to perform pilgrimage and had no intentions for fighting. After negotiating back and forth, the truce of Hudaybiyyah was signed by both groups. The treaty between the Muslims and the idol-worshippers of Quraish in Mecca stated that there would be no fighting between the two parties for ten years. And if any other tribe in Arabia wishes to join allegiance with the Muslims or idol-worshippers of Quraish, they may do so. No side is allowed to attack the other side, including the tribes that join the treaty. The treaty also stated that Prophet Muhammad and the Muslims were to return to Medina without performing Umrah and that they would be able to perform the Umrah pilgrimage the following year and stay for three days. The treaty also stated that if anyone leaves Mecca to go to Medina, he would be sent back to Mecca, even if he converted to Islam. But if a Muslim leaves Medina to go to Mecca, he does not need to be sent back.

The companions did not like the terms of the treaty, as it seemed unfavorable to them, and they were disappointed. Yet the Prophet accepted, honored, and abided by the treaty. Some of the companions spoke up to Prophet Muhammad, peace be upon him. They asked the Prophet *'Where is the victory that we were promised?'* and he was asked, *'Didn't you say we were going to perform pilgrimage?'* in which Prophet Muhammad, peace be upon him, responded, *'Yes, but I never said it was this year.'*

During the return journey from Hudaybiyyah, God the Almighty revealed a Chapter in the Holy Quran named *'Al-Fath (The Victory).'* God revealed that this truce was indeed a great victory for the Muslims. With this new treaty, the religion of Islam was able to flourish in the

Arabian Peninsula and spread rapidly. The Muslims went from having 1,400 men in this gathering to 10,000 men, two years later, to liberate Makkah. A lot of good happened in the two years after this treaty was signed. The Muslims were able to eliminate other threats, including the tribe of Khaybar. The Muslims also battled the Romans, the mighty superpower of the world at the time. Prophet Muhammad, peace be upon him, also sent letters to the kings beyond Arabia, calling them to Islam, including the King of Persia, the Negus of Abyssinia, the Emperor of Byzantium, the Governor of Egypt, and others - inviting them to submit to Islam.

The Conquest of Makkah

Over the next year or two, different surrounding tribes joined either the Muslim's side or the side of the idol-worshippers of Mecca. One of the tribes that joined the idol-worshippers side was the tribe of Bakr, and one of the tribes that joined the Muslim side was the tribe of Banu Khuzaʿah. Both of these tribes did not like each other and had a history of fighting with each other.

The tribe of Bakr, from the idol-worshippers side, asked permission from Meccan idol-worshippers if they could attack and confiscate the belongings of the tribe of Khuzaʿah, even though that would go against the treaty. The idol-worshippers of Mecca allowed it and even provided them with some weapons to earn a share of the profits they were going to confiscate. The idol-worshippers of Mecca advised the tribe of Bakr to attack the tribe of Khuzaʿah in the middle of the night, so no one can see them and so the Muslims would not find out.

After the attack, the news reached Prophet Muhammad and the Muslims. The idol-worshippers got nervous and decided to send their leader Abu Sufyan to talk to Prophet Muhammad, peace be upon him, and ask for the existing treaty to be renewed. However, Prophet Muhammad, peace be upon him, did not assure him that the treaty was still valid because they had broken the treaty.

After this event, Prophet Muhammad, peace be upon him, and the Muslims raised a big army of 10,000 men to surprise attack the idol-worshippers in Mecca for what they did. When the Muslims reached Mecca, the people of Mecca were overwhelmed and unable to fight the Muslims. Prophet Muhammad, peace be upon him, did not fight them and offered safety and security for anyone that did not fight. He announced to the people of Mecca that anyone who stays in the Kaaba, or their homes, or in the home of Abu Sufiyan—their leader who ended up converting to Islam, would be safe.

Prophet Muhammad, peace be upon him, entered Mecca with his head bowed down in humility, his head touching the back of his camel. He also circulated the Kaaba. Prophet Muhammad and the Muslims, peace be upon them, conquered the city of Mecca in a bloodless battle. This was the end of many years of persecution.

Prophet Muhammad, peace be upon him, gathered the people of Mecca and asked them, *'After all the evil things you did, what do you think I should do to you?'* They sought forgiveness, and Prophet Muhammad, peace be upon him, responded with the same phrase as Prophet Joseph said to his brothers, *'No blame or harm will be upon you today, Allah will forgive you.'* Then Prophet Muhammad, peace be upon him, freed the people of Mecca to go their separate way.

Then he ordered every idol in Kaaba to be destroyed, and he participated in destroying all 360 idols. Prophet Muhammad, peace be upon him, would point at an idol, and it would fall to the ground. The Kaaba was purified of all idols. Prophet Muhammad then ordered Bilal, peace be upon him, who had a strong melodious voice, to call the Adhan— which became the first Adhan in Islamic history from the Kaaba-- proclaiming the worship of the One the Only True God.

The Farewell Hajj

After Makkah had been conquered, Prophet Muhamad and many of his companions returned to Medina. It was the 9th year of the Hijrah— known as the *'Year of the Delegations'* since each tribe from all over the Arabian Peninsula sent a group of representatives to greet Prophet Muhammad to declare their allegiance and pledge their commitment to him. Prophet Muhammad and his companions, peace be upon them, hosted the groups of representatives in the Prophet's Mosque in Medina. The representatives of each tribe heard the Holy Quran being recited, watched the companions pray, and learned about Islam from Prophet Muhamad, peace be upon him.

Many of the representatives believed in the Message immediately and were satisfied, and some did not accept as smoothly as the others. The representatives of the tribes returned to their people, calling them to accept Islam, teaching them what they'd learned and telling them they needed to get rid of all their idols. Eventually, the whole Arabian Peninsula had accepted Islam.

In the 10th year of the Hijrah, Allah, the Glorious, revealed a command to perform Hajj for those capable of doing so. Prophet Muhammad, peace be upon him, announced that he was going to perform Hajj Pilgrimage to Mecca. Flocks of people—tens of thousands of people from all over joined him—it was the largest gathering in the Arabian Peninsula at the time.

Throughout the Hajj pilgrimage, Prophet Muhammad gave several sermons, including the famous primary sermon-- on the day of Arafat from the plain of Arafat (Mount of Mercy). There, he declared equality and solidarity between all the Muslims and reminded them of all the duties Islam had enjoined them upon. He forbade stealing, killing people, involvement in interest, and more. He commanded everyone to be good and just to their wives and women. He relayed the famous words to them of *'There is no superiority of an Arab over a non-Arab nor of a non-Arab over an Arab, nor a white over a black, nor a black over a white, except by taqwa (piety, fear of God, & God conciseness).'*

He told them there are two things if they hold on to, they will not go astray-- and that is the Book of Allah; The Holy Quran and the Sunnah; the teachings of the last and final Prophet, Muhammad peace be upon him. He reminded them that they would return to their Lord one day who will judge them based on their deeds. In the end, he asked them, *'Have I not conveyed the Message?'* The companions replied *'Yes!'* Then Prophet Muhammad raised his hands in the air and looked up into the sky and said three times, *'O Allah you bear witness!'*

Prophet Muhammad Returns to Medina & Passes Away

Soon after, Prophet Muhammad, peace be upon him, returned to the city of Medina. Prophet Muhammad received his final Revelation from God. Now that the faith of Islam was well established among his people and his community, his mission was coming to an end.

Soon after that, Prophet Muhammad, peace be upon him, fell ill for 10 to 12 days or so as his fever worsened in the house of his wife Aisha, peace be upon her, the mother of the believers. His body would get hot, and Aisha, peace be upon her, would recite Quran over him and cool him off with a wet towel.

He then sadly passes away on the lap of his wife, Aisha, peace be upon her. His companions were in shock and very sad about this tragedy. He was buried in the exact place he died, and his companions prayed for him individually.

Today, millions of Muslims go to Medina and send their salutations to our blessed Prophet. In the Holy Quran, God states that He did not send Prophet Muhammad, peace be upon him, except as a mercy for humanity. His role as the leader of the Islamic State was taken over by Abu Bakr, peace be upon him.

You are encouraged to visit the various posts and videos featured on The Sincere Seeker Blog on *https://www.thesincereseeker.com* or on The Sincere Seeker's YouTube Channel. You are also encouraged to subscribe to The Sincere Seeker Newsletter and YouTube Channel, to be notified when a new post or video is available for review.

For questions or comments, contact The Sincere Seeker at *hello@thesincereseeker.com*

Printed in Dunstable, United Kingdom